How to Easily Turn Everyday Activities into Learning Adventures for Kids

What People Are Saying

When I was first given a copy of *PLUS IT!* I didn't really see what help it could be. Surely this information was obvious. But then I read it! I was completely inspired. The ideas and suggestions are so creative and so easy to incorporate into the daily routine. I pretty much read it from start to finish in one sitting. It made me realize how rich our world is and how much potential for learning there is all around us if we open our eyes and look. A really invaluable tool for anyone who spends time with children.

—Virginia Fraser, Consultant,
Dunsfold, England

I'm giving a copy to my husband! *PLUS IT!* is on the mark. The strategies are really special. They build vocabulary, thinking, observation, self-awareness, responsibility, gratitude, and so much more. Using the book will create developmentally healthy interaction and dialogue between caregiver and child. I love it.

—Elizabeth Bloom, Educator,
Los Angeles, CA

PLUS IT! is a quick, easy read. I love the hands-on approach, and I can see myself using it to complement the materials I've developed for parent workshops. I give *PLUS IT!* an A+!

—Andrea Patten, LADC, Co-author,
What Kids Need to Succeed: Four Foundations of Adult Achievement
• www.whatkidsneedtosucceed.com • NH

PLUS IT! is a wealth of refreshing ideas. As an elementary school teacher, I use them with students while waiting in line and during short breaks. As a mother of a five-year-old, I use them to make everyday activities exciting and educational and to promote creativity. I love how quick, effective, and easy it is to use this book.

—Christine O'Donnell,
Second Grade Bilingual Teacher, Lennox, CA

I highly recommend *PLUS IT!* for anyone who cares about their child's well being. It has memory-making ideas with easy 'how to' steps every family can and should use to help build healthy bodies and sharp, inquisitive minds.

—Pat Burns, Author,
*Grandparents Rock: The Grandparenting
Guide for the Rock-n-Roll Generation.*
Co-founder of the Orange County
Children's Book Festival, CA

As I read *PLUS IT!* I thought of all the things I wish I'd done with my children. Now as a senior, it's opened up my mind to what I could do for my own learning. It's vivid. It flows. I love that it's so interactive. I can see myself doing these things, and I wish I had kids around to inspire them with these ideas. If only parents would do these easy and fun things!

—Marla Keesee, Registrar (retired),
University of Santa Monica, CA

How to Easily Turn Everyday Activities into Learning Adventures for Kids

Esther Jantzen

New York

Plus It!

How to Easily Turn Everyday Activities Into Learning Adventures for Kids

Cover design by ImageOneAds.com

Library of Congress Control Number: 2008943935

Library of Congress Cataloging-in-Publication Data
Jantzen, Esther A., 1945-
Plus it! How to easily turn everyday activities into learning adventures for kids/
Esther Jantzen
ISBN 978-1-60037-566-8 (paperback)
1. Parenting. 2. Child rearing. 3. Early childhood. 4. Family and relationships. I. Title.

MORGAN · JAMES
THE ENTREPRENEURIAL PUBLISHER

Morgan James Publishing, LLC
1225 Franklin Ave., STE 325
Garden City, NY 11530-1693
Toll Free 800-485-4943
www.MorganJamesPublishing.com

For two of the great loves of my life,
Rowan Helena Glenn and Colin Wyatt Glenn

Acknowledgments

To those who have supported me on the multiple entrepreneurial adventures I've undertaken in the past few years—thank you, thank you for the advice, cheerleading, editing, feedback, ideas, inspiration, and other vital assistance you have given me:

Cristina Abad, Robert Allen, Tom Antion, Diane Carty-Speicher, Susan Curington, Sheriden DeWees, Virginia Farrington, Jeanette Fisher, Ann Folks, Ginny Fraser, Bernadette Jantzen Glenn and Clayton Glenn, Robert Gould, Jennifer Halet, Suzanne Turner Hanifl, Mark Victor Hansen and the Mega Inner Circle, Dan and Betty Jantzen, Jim and Susan Jantzen, Jon and Mary Beth Jantzen, Tillie and Lubin Jantzen, Marla Keesee, Jan Keiser, Terri Levine, Mark Little, Pat Lund, Frankie Mamone, Karina Martens, Ann McIndoo, Shelley Noble, Lois Palio, Paula Paul, Gwen Perrone, Cece Pinkerton, Kathleen S. Ralph, Joann Reeves, Kathe Robbs, John-Roger and John Morton, Eileen Senner, Mary Jo Tate, Julie Viskup, Corrie Woods, Joann Yabrof—and oh, so many more.

I love, bless, thank, and honor you from the bottom of my heart!

Contents

Acknowledgments ix

Introduction xv

1. Getting Started: Ten Ways to PLUS IT! with
   Ordinary Activities 1

   How to Use This Book • Make It a Game • Describe It
   • Plan It Out Loud • Write It Down • Time It—How
   Long Does It Take? • Collect It—For a Week, a Month,
   a Year, or a Lifetime • Report It—Something Pleasant
   in the Day • Draw It—Make a Picture • Compare It •
   Decorate It

2. PLUS IT! on a Walk 15

   Count Something as You Walk • Listen for Something
   • Clean Up Something • Make Up a Walking Song
   • Estimate Distances • Look for Shapes in Clouds •
   Play "I Spy" • Investigate Shadows • Different Ways of
   Walking • Find Beautiful Things • How Many Color
   Shades?

3. PLUS IT! while You Wait: Nine Great Things
   for Kids to Memorize 25

   Local Geography and Politics • States and Capitals •
   Common Nursery Rhymes • Song Lyrics • Common
   Phrases in a New Language • Religious Verses and Prayers
   • Favorite Poems • Trees, Shrubs, and Common Flowers
   • Sports, Hobby, or Special Interest Information

4. PLUS IT! for the Mind: Nine Ways to
    Stretch the Imagination 33

    Play "Someday I Want" • Play "If I Were" or "What
    If" • Play Pretend "When I Become" • Play "If I
    Could" • Play "Here's a Problem. What's a Solution?"
    • Play "What's Going on Here" • Make Up a Story
    and Solution • Three Wishes • Use Something in an
    Unusual Way: "What Could We Make?"

5. PLUS IT! with Low Moods: Fifteen Things
    to Do When Kids Are Feeling Blue. 43

    Breathe Deeply • Finish Something That's Been Started
    • Acknowledge and Accept It • Do Something Nice for
    Someone Else • Say "I'm Sorry," Forgive Yourself, and
    Then Forget • Be Grateful • Refocus—What Could
    Be Good about This? • Experience Nature • Express
    It—Write about It • A TV Show in Your Mind: Visualize
    Something Good • Laugh about It • Move and Exercise
    • Get or Give a Hug • Rest • Think of Three Things You
    Want to Do

6. PLUS IT! Without Money: When Kids Want
    to Spend It and You Don't 53

    Find the Free Things • Play Indoor and Table Games
    • Start a Small Business • Organize Physical Activities
    • Do an Act of Service • Plan a No-Cost Party • Learn
    Survival Skills • Use the Public Library Services • Plan a
    Spend-No-Money Day or Weekend • Have a Scavenger
    Hunt

7. PLUS IT! with TV and Technology. 61

    Characters You Like • Act As If, Impersonate, Pretend,
    and Make Believe • Retell • Retell and Revise • My
    Strategies • Winning and Losing • Help 'Em Out

8. PLUS IT! for Housework: Fun with Dirt and
    "Drudgery"................................67

    Make a List • The Fun of Finishing • A Place for
    Everything • Health and Housework: How These
    Things Relate • Make Life Easier: The Right Tool •
    Maintaining Tools and Equipment • Caring for Plants
    • Caring for Pets

9. PLUS IT! with Decisions: Ten Questions to
    Teach Kids to Ask........................77

10. PLUS IT! in a Car: Ten Ways to Use Travel
    Time....................................79

    Books on Tape, CD, iPods, or Other Players •
    Observation Games • Backseat Read-Aloud • Backseat
    Navigator • How Far? • Fill 'er Up! • Car Care • Bus,
    Train, or Subway Options • What's Around Here •
    Highway Reporter

11. PLUS IT! at the Table: Supper Conversation
    Starters.................................87

12. Do It Yourself: Three Easy Steps to Creating
    PLUS IT! Activities......................91

    How to Transform Ordinary Activities into Educational
    Ones • Notice • Talk and Listen • PLUS IT!—Do
    Something Deliberate with the Activity

BONUS OFFER!..............................97

About the Author..........................99

❖   ❖   ❖

Nothing done for children is ever wasted.
—Garrison Keillor

❖   ❖   ❖

Introduction

Have you ever asked yourself, "Hmm ... What will I do with the kids today?" If so, this book can help you out.

This is a lighthearted guidebook for creating happy moments with kids. I want to share with you a perspective on how to add value and fun to many of the things you do every day.

I wrote it because when I was a single parent with a demanding teaching job, I often wondered—How can I get through this day, do all the things I need to do, handle the housework, and still give my daughter the experiences she needs to learn and grow? And how can we have fun together in the process?

When you're in a house with restless children and don't want to stick them in front of the television, what can you do with them? And when you're in the midst of those child-tending days that sometimes drag, what can you do to enjoy them and stay pleasant?

Now, as a grandparent, I see all sorts of easy opportunities I missed back then because I just hadn't thought of these ideas! And now, as a grandparent, I know how quickly those child-rearing years go. Bam! The kids are grown. What happened? What did I miss?

Often we hear that being a parent, or someone who takes care of children, is the most important job in the world. But truth be told, parents and caregivers don't get much support. I hope this book provides some for you, because it's true, your parenting job is most important. Please know that I appreciate and honor you for being willing to care for a child.

All the chapters of this book are short. It starts with an overview of how to use it and ten general ways you can PLUS your everyday tasks. Then each chapter addresses a different situation you probably have with your children. This book is not academic research or educational theory, but at various points I let you know the educational reasons behind some of the suggestions.

You can start reading *PLUS IT!* at any point, because it is more like a restaurant menu than a sequenced program of events. I invite you to write notes in your copy—check off the things you tried; jot down your own ideas at the end of a chapter. This book will have fulfilled its mission if you get several good ideas from it that you use in your daily life with children.

You're welcome to write me your success stories in using *PLUS IT!* ideas at the blog on www.plusitbook. com. Did your kids learn something from the activities? Did you and they enjoy them? I intend that this little volume will be the first in a series. Please be on the lookout for more!

Esther A. Jantzen, Ed.D.

Chapter 1

Getting Started:
Ten Ways to PLUS IT! with Ordinary Activities

❖　❖　❖

If you can give your son or daughter
only one gift, let it be enthusiasm.
—Bruce Barton

❖　❖　❖

Imagine helping kids get the advantage in school simply by adding an easy step to their normal activities at home.

Imagine your kids telling *their* kids, twenty-five years from now, "When I was growing up, my parents (or babysitter, aunt, uncle, grandma, grandpa) made games of the simplest things, and I learned so much!"

That's what I mean by *"PLUS-ing"* the activities of daily life. It's taking an idea or what you're already doing and making it a bit better.

There's no cost. Very little extra time is required. The benefits are fun, eagerness, and happy memories for children (and the adults who care for them). And you'll be confident you are helping children build attitudes and skills for lifelong success.

The *really important* thing here is to show them ways to learn from every experience. Teach them to get value from every problem, every situation, and every activity.

It may be the best training you can ever provide your children.

◆   ◆   ◆

Kids spell love T-I-M-E.
—John Crudele

◆   ◆   ◆

How to Use This Book

This chapter provides general ideas to get you started with *PLUS IT!* activities. It also explains ten ways to transform an ordinary activity into a learning opportunity. Chapters 2–11 offer lots of suggestions for specific situations. Shop through them, and see what attracts you.

Use these ideas as a springboard. Tweak them, adapt them, or expand on them for your own situation. Invent and create even more fun things to do. Chapter 12 provides ideas for creating your own *PLUS IT!* activities.

Try them with kids under the age of ten. Some ideas here are for preschoolers, some for elementary kids. Modify them if they are too hard or too easy for your children. What's important is to challenge kids, but not to frustrate them. Go for the fun of learning together!

Use this book as a workbook—well, actually, as a playbook. Jot down ideas, and make notes in the margin or in the space provided at the end of each chapter. Record dates that you tried something. Keep this book where you can reach it easily.

When possible, write down your kids' responses. Why? Because it teaches observation skills and makes you, and them, more aware of what works and what doesn't. (If this suggestion is too burdensome, though, forget it. Just do these activities in whatever way works for you.)

Prepare a Creativity Box. A large cardboard box or plastic container with a lid works fine. Put the supplies listed below into it, and keep it where children can reach it easily.

* Writing paper—lined and unlined
* Pens, pencils, markers, crayons
* Blunt scissors, school glue, tape
* A few envelopes

Other helpful things to have in your home (optional):

* A digital timer
* A three-hole punch
* A three-ring binder

◆ ◆ ◆

Many things we need can wait. The child cannot.
Now is the time his bones are being formed; his blood
is being made; his mind is being developed. To him we
cannot say tomorrow. His name is today.
—Gabriela Mistral

◆ ◆ ◆

Here are ten general ways to transform what you do on ordinary days into productive fun:

1. Make It a Game

You can make a game of something for kids by asking for a number, a guess, or a choice, or by making it a competition. Here are a few examples:

A mailbox game: Ask, "How many envelopes or flyers do you think we'll get in the mail today?" You can *PLUS* this by listing (or having your children list) the days of the week and the number of items that show up in the mailbox each day. Do that for two weeks or a month, then ask your children to notice if there's a pattern when the most or the fewest pieces of mail come. Let them guess why that might be.

A laundry game: If you and your child sort the dirty clothes by color, say, "Guess how many towels we have in that pile? How many T-shirts?" You can *PLUS* doing the laundry by having children measure the detergent, or pour it into the washer. Let the preschoolers help fold small items when they are dry.

A grocery store game: Ask your child, "Which picture on a carton (or can, box, or bottle) most makes you want to eat what's inside?" Or "As you walk the aisles, how many things do you see that you like to eat that begin with the letter 'P' [or the first letter of the child's name]?" To *PLUS* this, make a list with the child of all the food "P" items (or any letter of the alphabet) that the child likes, and add to it over time. This teaches phonetic awareness, observation, making choices, and determining preferences. It helps develop vocabulary and spelling, too.

2. Describe It

When we describe what we see or experience, we first have to observe it, and then use precise words.

Imagine you're walking with a two-year-old child who points to a dog across the street and exclaims, "Doggie!" You can respond with descriptive words, "Yes, that's a large dog with shaggy, golden-brown and white hair. It's a collie."

Model for the child the habit of noticing details, and don't hesitate to use big words or the proper names of things with children. They learn words by hearing you use them. For example, when paying for something at the supermarket, you might say, "I'm going to pay today in currency rather than using a debit card." Thus kids learn that "currency" is another word for cash or paper money.

Prompt older children to give details. When they say, "Mom, look at that candleholder," you can say something such as, "Yes, what I notice about it is the amber color. What do you notice about it?" (Of course, you can mention smell, size, movement, use, or anything else unique.)

You may wonder what is gained when kids give or hear description. The answer is increased vocabulary; more complex sentence construction; and increased experience with observation, drawing conclusions, making comparisons, and thinking skills. These are great skills for building success in school.

3. Plan It Out Loud

In the presence of your child, say something such as, "Let's see, what do we need to do today? At 11:00, I have a doctor's appointment, so I'll need to leave at 10:20 for that. Then I need to call the landlord to fix the faucet. At 3:00, I'll pick you up, and you can come to the grocery store with me."

Then take a piece of paper and write down your schedule. This teaches children the habit of planning and recording appointments and agreements. It helps them learn to get places on time, and accomplish what's important.

An extension of this is to let your children dictate their schedules to you, or write them down themselves.

4. Write It Down

When you write things down, you show children the value of the written word. Once you have a collection place, such as a three-ring binder where you can put papers, established in your home, it only takes a few minutes.

What sorts of things should you write down? Things you don't want to forget, such as:

* Cute things your children say
* Ideas for gifts
* Books you hear about and want to read
* TV programs you don't want to miss
* Sales you hear about
* Grocery and shopping lists
* To-dos

5. Time It—How Long Does It Take?

The point of timing activities is to become aware of time, not to rush or race to get things done fast. Let your children guess how long something will take, and then time that activity.

For example, say, "I wonder how long it will take to do the dishes." Or "How long do you think it takes for us to walk around the block?" Or "I wonder how long it takes for the dog to finish his food, or for you to do your math homework." Or "How long do you think it will take to pick up your toys?"

This helps children who are learning to tell time understand the common time intervals—ten minutes, half an hour, an hour, and so forth. It helps older children focus, and learn where their time goes.

Setting a digital timer for twenty minutes or half an hour of reading can be another easy way to communicate time, plus fit some reading into your day.

6. Collect It—For a Week, a Month, a Year, or a Lifetime

Collecting can be done with a wide range of things. For example, do you have a pocket or purse full of change? Tell your children, "This week, let's collect pennies and see how many different dates we can find on the pennies."

In the course of the week, have your child line up the pennies on a table or windowsill in chronological order by the date on the coin. If your child wants to continue this after a week, find a place or way to do this.

Other ideas of things to collect from an ordinary day: stamps from envelopes, pictures from ads, postcards, bottle caps. You can probably think of more. Collecting something helps a child learn to group, categorize, and sequence things, which are important thinking skills.

Always find a reasonable place or container for children's collections, and get them to put the items there. Otherwise you'll have a mess on your hands.

7. Report It—Something Pleasant in the Day

There are many ways to do this. You can say something such as, "You know something I enjoyed today? It was taking a walk with you and seeing the irises in the neighbor's yard." Or "Do you know something nice that happened to me today in the grocery store? The person in front of me in the line told me about a really great movie to see. It was fun to hear about that."

If you work outside the home, you can say, "Today in our office …" or "Driving home today I saw a beautiful sunset," or "I heard a new song on the radio," or "The news reported something great today, and it was …"

This helps children become aware of what they're doing, and what's in their world. Ask them, "What's something good you noticed today?"

Talking about positive experiences generates gratitude. Gratitude promotes good feelings about one's self and others, cooperation, fun, good manners, and positive energy.

8. Draw It—Make a Picture

Drawing pictures activates a different part of our brain than talking does. It doesn't matter at all how the picture turns out; it only matters that you and/or your children do it!

Draw what? Anything. When you've completed an activity such as cleaning a bedroom, ask your children to draw a picture of it all cleaned up.

They can draw the living room, a bush on the street, the grandma who visited today, a bicycle they want, what's on the kitchen table, a chair. They can draw cars, space ships, animals, or anything from their fantasy life.

Ask your children to talk about their drawings. Write what they say on the back of the picture.

Save the pictures in a file folder or a pocket folder for each child.

9. Compare It

Important thinking skills are developed when you ask children to compare two or more things. You can do this in many ways throughout a day. For example, when you're doing the laundry with a child nearby, you could ask, "Which T-shirt is dirtier (or whiter)?"

When you're cooking, you might ask, "Which bottle or can has the most juice in it?" or "Do you think this leftover will fit into this container?"

When you're dressing children or picking out clothes, ask, "Which top is a brighter color?" "Which pants are longer?" "Which pajamas will be warmer— the ones with the feet or the ones without?"

10. Decorate It

Everyone enjoys something beautiful—even if we disagree on what beauty is. Taking a little extra time to figure out how to decorate or arrange something is gratifying and fun.

This is easy to do with food. For example, when you serve a heap of macaroni and cheese to a child, put something colorful on top—a few peas or beans, perhaps. Or ask the child what might make a good decoration on top of a bowl of oatmeal or cereal (raisins? walnuts?).

When you slice a banana, arrange the slices on the plate in the shape of a flower. Put a few flowers in a glass on the kitchen table, or fold the paper napkins in an unusual way.

Asking your children to think of ways to decorate stimulates creativity, imagination, and appreciation for simple things.

A child's room or sleeping area can be decorated with pictures, artwork, books, toys, and stuffed animals. Invite children to change things around in their rooms from time to time. Encourage using simple, ordinary things to make a space attractive.

These are a few general ways you can *PLUS IT!* with normal household activities and make them stimulating, fun, and educational.

Kids are easily influenced by their parent's or caregiver's enthusiasm and encouragement. Let those two qualities flow from you. They support kids in learning and growing intellectually and emotionally for years.

❖   ❖   ❖

Education is not preparation for life;
education is life itself.
—John Dewey

❖   ❖   ❖

Add your own ideas below:

_____

_____

_____

_____

_____

_____

_____

_____

_____

_____

Chapter 2

PLUS IT! on a Walk

For thousands of years, people have been taking walks for entertainment, exercise, shopping, running errands, thinking and meditating, and just to get from one place to another.

Do you need an excuse to take a walk with kids? Here are a few: walk the dog on a leash, visit the neighbors, go to a store, stretch your legs, improve a mood, breathe fresh air, walk off a big meal, and give kids a chance to run freely.

The ideas you'll find in this chapter for taking walks that are both fun and informative are mostly for use with kids under age ten. Older children may enjoy them, too, and you can adapt them to their interests, or create new ones.

❖   ❖   ❖

Learn everything you can, anytime you can, from anyone you can—there will always come a time when you will be grateful you did.
—Sarah Caldwell

❖   ❖   ❖

1. Count Something as You Walk

Children have an endless fascination with numbers. Preschool and early elementary kids may be proud of how high they can count—and when you tell them to just add one more to their highest number, they're off and counting again. Older children can be challenged to estimate how many of something there are—how many people in an auditorium, how many cans on a shelf.

So when you're on a walk with a child—perhaps walking the dog, visiting a neighbor, or going to a park or library—use the walk experience to play with numbers. For example, ask your child:

* ❋ How many houses do we pass?
* ❋ How many dogs do we see?
* ❋ How many windows in that apartment building?
* ❋ How many sycamore trees (or any trees) on the block?
* ❋ How many steps from one lamppost to another?

* How many telephone poles?
* How many people say hello when we greet them?
* How many cement squares are in the sidewalk?

2. Listen for Something

Children are often very aware of sounds, perhaps more aware than adults who may tune them out. Directing them to use their ears in a deliberate way strengthens their ability to focus and develops sensory awareness.

For example, ask, "How many different animal sounds do you think we'll hear today in our neighborhood?"

Here are more ideas of things to listen for:

* Motor sounds (car, lawnmower, motorcycle, diesel engine, etc.)
* Bird sounds
* Sounds of different living things (insects, dogs, people)
* The wind
* Human voices
* The total number of different sounds (human, animal, mechanical, etc.)

Focus several walks on sounds. Take a pencil and a piece of paper or notepad with you, and write down what you hear.

3. Clean Up Something

Cleaning up may not appeal to everybody. However, it teaches important concepts about social responsibility, such as leaving a place better than you found it and that we all can help create beautiful communities.

Simply take a plastic or paper bag and a pair of work or household gloves with you when you go out on your walk. Together with the children, be alert for litter—bits of paper, bottles, and cans. Let your child spy the items, and then you can pick them up *using gloves* for protection.

If your neighborhood has more trash than you can pick up in a day, pick up one bag's worth each time you walk. Be sure to dispose of your trash bag properly.

4. Make Up a Walking Song

No one needs to be a great singer in order to enjoy singing. It doesn't matter whether you or your children can carry a tune. What you're going for is the fun!

Pick a common tune that children know such as "Old MacDonald Had a Farm" or "Twinkle, Twinkle, Little Star."

Then make up a song to that tune, using the names and situations you find yourself in. If you can make words rhyme, great. If not, that's just fine, too!

For example, using the Old MacDonald tune:

Little Robert took a walk, E-I-E-I-O

And on this walk he heard an ambulance, E-I-E-I-O.

With a wee-rre-[siren sound] here and a wee-rre-[siren sound] there ...

And so on through the song.

Let yourselves be silly! You can play this game with almost any tune.

5. Estimate Distances

This activity develops arithmetic skills and is good for children who love counting. It's easy, and it gives experience with estimating, which is an important skill related to understanding numbers.

Ask your child, "How many steps do you think there are from here (wherever you are standing) to the corner (or some other point you name)?"

Then walk the distance, counting steps, and compare the answer with your guess. It doesn't matter if the guess is right or not. We learn from the experience of trying.

6. Look for Shapes in Clouds

On a day with floating clouds in the sky, play "Let's Look for Shapes." You can look for animal shapes or geometric shapes. You might say, "I see a cloud that is shaped like an oval (or a duck)" and see if the child can find it. Take turns in selecting a cloud to describe.

If you want to take this a step further, look up cloud types in a book or on the Internet, and learn their names.

7. Play "I Spy"

Play "I Spy with My Little Eye." One person picks out an object that everyone can see, and says, without naming the object, "I spy with my little eye something that's red," or "I spy with my little eye something that begins with the letter *p*."

Then the others look around and name red things (or things that begin with *p*): "Is it the bow on the wreath on the neighbor's door?" The person who guesses correctly gets to make the next pick. It's a simple way to teach new words.

8. Investigate Shadows

This works best on a sunny day. The experience of noticing and understanding what creates a shadow can turn a child on to the wonders of the heavens. Here are some ways to do this:

* Stand together with children with your backs to the sun, and see who has the longest or shortest shadow. Why is that?
* Play "Step on My Shadow" to experiment with how you have to move to avoid having your shadow stepped on.

✳ Notice the shadow of a tree, bush, or building, and mark a spot on the ground for its edge. Return later in the day and notice how the edge of the shadow has moved. Why is that?

✳ Ask, "Are shadows real?" Hmm. Interesting question!

✳ Using your hands, make shadow figures. (You can find amazing examples on the Internet. Search for "hand shadows.")

✳ When you get home, ask your child to draw a picture of a person with a shadow. Where would the sun have to be in the picture to create the shadow?

9. Different Ways of Walking

How many different ways of walking or running can you and the children invent? Take along an index card, make up a name for each way of walking, and write them down. For example:

✳ Walk like a duck, feet turned outward
✳ Skip
✳ Walk like a pigeon, feet turned inward
✳ Hop
✳ Walk backwards
✳ Walk sideways
✳ Take tiny steps
✳ Take large steps

* Gallop like a horse
* Walk like you have a stone in your shoe
* March like in a parade band
* Dance like a ballerina

10. Find Beautiful Things

This is fun because it trains your eye to look for things you think are beautiful. People don't have to agree about what's beautiful.

Ask, "What do you see around us that's beautiful to you?" Answers might be:

* I see a small smooth gray stone, and I think it's a beautiful shape.
* I see a large pointy brown leaf on the ground, and I think it's a beautiful color.
* I see a tree branch waving in the breeze, and I think that movement is beautiful.

11. How Many Color Shades?

Colors come in many different shades and hues, and it's fun to notice them, and decide which you like best. On one walk with a child, look for all the different hues of green (or any color) you see, and make up names for them, such as pine-tree green, cactus green, fresh-grass green, blue-green, fire-hydrant red, bright-door red, or summer-sky blue.

When you get home, see if you can find the standard names for those color hues. Check the names in a box of crayons or colored pencils, use the Internet to find color names, or get a library book on colors. What shades do you love most? Periwinkle? Magenta?

Add your own ideas for things you can do on a walk:

_____

_____

_____

_____

_____

_____

_____

_____

_____

_____

_____

_____

_____

_____

_____

_____

Chapter 3

PLUS IT! while You Wait:
Nine Great Things for Kids to Memorize

You can make use of the time spent with children in the car, in waiting rooms, or in lines by memorizing interesting or useful information.

Children love to tell the things they know by heart. Preschoolers happily sing the alphabet song, or say the numbers one to ten or to one- hundred. They love to recite nursery rhymes, jump-rope rhymes, songs, simple prayers, and poems. They feel proud to know foreign language phrases or numbers. Older children proudly share specialized knowledge about science, history, people, sports, or other topics that they learn in school, through the media, or from elsewhere.

If children hear or see something frequently, they'll memorize it almost automatically. Make it a game to memorize things. It's especially fun to memorize along with others—kids can prompt each other, quiz each other, and race each other.

Things committed to memory at a young age stay with us for a lifetime. They can be both useful and comforting. Perhaps you've used the "i before e" rhyme to help you spell correctly, or you've sung all the verses to a carol or a folk song, or you've prayed the Lord's Prayer or another ritual prayer as you buried a pet fish. Give your children the gift of knowing these things, too.

Write down on a card or sheet of paper what you want your children to memorize. Carry it with you and pull it out when an opportunity presents itself.

But first be sure your children memorize the information they may need in emergency situations: their address, parents' or caregivers' names, and important telephone numbers (including cell phone numbers).

Also, when children are given assignments to memorize something at school—such as the times tables, the planets, or a song—support their efforts enthusiastically. Make those assignments a priority, and make them fun.

Here are some additional things for kids to memorize:

1. Local Geography and Politics

* The country we live in
* The state we live in
* The capital of our state

* The county we live in
* The town (or city) we live in
* The section of town we live in
* The street we live on

If a child is old enough and loves this sort of thing, add knowledge about politicians who represent you. You might learn a thing or two yourself!

* The president of our country
* The governor of our state
* The senators of our state
* The representative from our area
* The mayor of our town (or city)

2. States and Capitals

Children in early and middle grades often enjoy learning all the states and their capitals—there are fifty of them. Again, you might learn along with them! Make flashcards with the state name on one side and the capital on the other. Carry them in the car or in a purse. Use a map or United States jigsaw puzzle to learn the locations of the states.

3. Common Nursery Rhymes

Nursery rhymes are part of our culture, and children benefit from knowing them. They teach rhyme, rhythm, vocabulary, and common images. Every child needs to know that "Mary Had a Little Lamb," that "Jack and Jill Went Up a Hill" together, and that "Humpty Dumpty Sat on a Wall."

Libraries carry Mother Goose books, and reading these rhymes aloud to children helps them learn them quickly. Jump-rope, jacks, and street games rhymes are also wonderful for kids to learn by heart.

4. Song Lyrics

It's fun to know the correct words to songs you love, whether they are popular songs, folk songs, carols, lullabies, hymns, patriotic songs, musicals, or any other songs. Do you know all the words to "The Star Spangled Banner" or "America the Beautiful"?

You can find lyrics via an Internet search. Write them on a card, and carry them with you until you learn them.

Then sing your favorite songs loud and clear in the car, at home, on walks, anywhere—and have fun doing it!

5. Common Phrases in a New Language

Do you want your children to learn Spanish? French? Some other language? Get a phrase book from the language of your choice, and carry it in the car. Quiz one another as you run errands.

Language CDs are available in libraries, bookstores, and sometimes at garage sales. Use these to help get the right pronunciation and to learn even more.

6. Religious Verses and Prayers

Part of our country's culture comes from our religious traditions and sacred scriptures—from the Bible, the Talmud, the Koran, or other writings. Scriptural passages are referred to often in literature and politics, and knowing them helps us understand and appreciate speeches and written works.

You and your children may get satisfaction from memorizing the most famous passages.

7. Favorite Poems

Like nursery rhymes, certain poems are standard knowledge in our society. For example, your children may have fun memorizing limericks such as "An Old Person from Ware" by Edward Lear, or short poems such as "In January" by Maurice Sendak, and "The Pancake" by Christina Rossetti.

Don't forget finger play and movement songs such as "Did You Ever See a Lassie," "Five Little Monkeys Jumping on the Bed," "Hush Little Baby," "Kookaburra," "Oats, Peas, Beans, and Barley Grow," "Oh Where, Oh Where Has My Little Dog Gone?" "One Potato, Two Potato," and "Where Is Thumbkin?"

8. Trees, Shrubs, and Common Flowers

Children who can identify the common plants in their geographic region develop a respect for the environment, an interest in science, and greater observation skills.

Of course, you have to be able to identify them yourself if you want kids to know them! If you are not strong in this area, you and your children can learn the names at stores that sell plants or through books that show common plants. Sometimes there's nothing a neighbor or relative would rather do than to introduce you and your children to the flowers in their garden.

If you're going to have trouble remembering plant names, write them down.

9. Sports, Hobby, or Special Interest Information

Many kids are proud to know and share all sorts of information related to sports teams, games, and exceptional athletes; to their hobbies; or to their special interests.

Encourage these interests, for they help kids develop reading skills, focus, and an understanding of the larger world.

❖   ❖   ❖

Children without words are licked before they start.
—Peter S. Jennison

❖   ❖   ❖

Add your own ideas below of great things to memorize:

_____

_____

_____

_____

_____

_____

_____

_____

_____

_____

_____

_____

_____

_____

_____

_____

_____

_____

Chapter 4

❖   ❖   ❖

To invent, you need a good imagination
and a pile of junk.
—Thomas Edison

❖   ❖   ❖

Our imaginations lead us to create stories, movies, buildings, inventions, toys, tools, wealth, games, gifts, relationships, and oh-so-much more. In fact, just about everything we see in the world is the result of people first using their imaginations.

Imagination is an incredibly valuable asset that every child (and every adult) has.

❖   ❖   ❖

Nothing happens unless first we dream.
—Carl Sandburg

❖   ❖   ❖

Some kids have wild imaginations and may scare themselves when they imagine things such as monsters in shadows. (If this becomes a problem for your children, show them how they can just as easily imagine protectors or solutions to what scares them.)

Other children need to be encouraged to imagine—especially to imagine good things for their future. Psychologists tell us that when we just imagine or see ourselves doing or being something specific, we begin the process of creating that, or perhaps something better, in our lives.

What follows is a list of ways to *PLUS IT!* with imagination—to direct a child's thoughts in happy ways. You can do these activities in the car, while waiting in line, or anywhere else. Some of the starter sentences are quite similar to one another. Choose the ones that make sense in your situation.

As you play with children with the ideas below, simply appreciate what the kids come up with. You don't need to improve or fix or even add to their ideas. Simply accepting their ideas stimulates brainstorming, creative thinking, and problem-solving. It can help them become flexible and open to new learning.

When possible, write down what each child mentions (and put the date on it), and add to it over time. If you do this occasionally over the course of a few years, you'll have a remarkable record of the development of your child's mind.

◆　◆　◆

Imagination is more important than knowledge.
Knowledge is limited. Imagination encircles the world.
　　　　　—Albert Einstein

◆　◆　◆

1. Play "Someday I Want"

When kids watch a TV program or video or read a book about an interesting place, you can *PLUS IT!* by inviting them to finish the sentence, "Someday I want to go to (or see) …" Then ask what other places they may want to visit. Real places or imaginary places—both are fine.

Let them know that if they imagine themselves there, the chances are good that someday they will find a way to visit, do, or see what they imagine. For example:

"Someday I want to go to Alaska and see polar bears."

"Someday I want to make a tree-house / a doll house / a car engine."

"Someday I want to learn to swim / ride a bike / speak a foreign language."

"Someday I want to have a car / a house / a job / a family / a business."

Write these "somedays" down!

2. Play "If I Were" or "What If"

"If I were a scientist, I'd discover ..."

"If I were Harry Potter (or the president, or God, or the boss of this house), I would ..."

"If I were a genie (or a fairy or a dog), I would ..."

"What if the world were flat?"

Use these sentence starters and questions to help kids imagine what it would be like to be someone other than who they are, or what it would be like if the world were different. This helps them experience what it's like to be in someone else's shoes. It helps build understanding. As they fill in the blanks with their ideas, you play, too. "If I were a millionaire ..." "If I were President ..." "What if we moved to the city (or the country or a new neighborhood)?"

3. Play Pretend "When I Become"

This sentence starter helps kids think of their future careers. For example, a child might say, "When I become a teacher, I'll take my class on lots of field trips. When I become a teacher, I'll make recess longer."

Let them know they are pretending, not making a promise or commitment. It doesn't matter if they change from day to day what they say they want to become. Each time they "try on" an idea, they begin to get a sense of whether it is what they really want or not.

4. Play "If I Could"

This sentence starter can be used for thinking about the present or the future. Here are suggestions to start with:

> "If I could get my homework finished in an hour …"

> "If I could invent a new car …"

> "If I could go to outer space …"

> "If I could go backward in time …"

> "If I could fly …"

> "If I could make world peace …"

5. Play "Here's a Problem. What's a Solution?"

Kids can invent amazing and fresh solutions to old problems. Their solutions don't have to be sensible or realistic. Some of the best solutions come from far-out ideas. Try asking your children these:

Here's the problem: Some people are homeless and live on the streets. What's a solution?

Here's the problem: We don't have a park in our neighborhood. What's a solution?

Here's the problem: We don't have enough money saved for a week's vacation. What's a solution?

❖   ❖   ❖

Creative problem-solving involves: fluency (creating lots of ideas); flexibility (accepting the possibility of more than one answer to a problem or more than one use for an object); originality (creating ideas which are unusual and different); and elaboration. When you take time to develop creative thinking with your children, you are helping them become happier and become better students.
—Stan Wonderley, *Success Starts Early*

❖   ❖   ❖

6. Play "What's Going on Here?"

Look at a picture of people doing something—a picture in a magazine, on a wall, in a book, or at a museum. Ask about or point out the details—the objects, the clothing, the colors. Ask, "What do you think the people in this picture were doing right before this scene (or right after this scene)?"

Because we don't really know the correct answer, accept any answer that makes some sense. Imagining what other people do is a way of creating fiction or making up stories.

7. Make Up a Story and Solution

This imagination stretcher is one you can play yourself, and invite your child to do it along with you. If your family or child has a concern, such as a bully in the neighborhood, make up a story with a character that has that same or a similar concern, and see if the character can figure out a good solution.

I remember a time when my young granddaughter was potty-trained but still resisted going to the bathroom. One day, before we started running a number of errands, I wanted her to go to the bathroom so she wouldn't have an accident while we were out. I made up a story for her about a brown puppy who wouldn't "go potty" when his master took him out on a walk. Of course, in the story, the first day that the puppy was left at home all day when the master went to work, the pup became very uncomfortable and almost had an accident in the house. Thus the next time he decided to "go" when taken on a walk. My granddaughter asked for that puppy story repeatedly. And, not surprisingly, her going-to-the-bathroom resistance changed, too. I wish I'd written the story down so we could have read it together.

8. Three Wishes

If you could have three wishes, and only those three, what would you choose? This question is a tricky one that has led many people into realizing that what they say they wish for isn't always what they really want. Write down the answers, and play this every few months to see if your answers change.

9. Use Something in an Unusual Way: "What Could We Make?"

What could children make with a small cardboard box? A large one? Plastic water bottles? Brown paper bags? A folded piece of paper? A heap of stones? A flower pot? An old tablecloth or blanket? Old newspapers? Empty tin cans without sharp edges? Egg cartons? A pack of index cards? Old birthday cards?

If possible, let them try making what they suggest.

◆　◆　◆

There are no Seven Wonders of the World in the eyes of a child. There are seven million.
—Walt Streightiff

Imagination is the highest kite one can fly.
—Lauren Bacall

◆　◆　◆

Add your own ideas for how to stretch the imagination:

_____

_____

_____

_____

_____

_____

❖ ❖ ❖

Man's mind, once stretched by a new idea, never regains its original dimensions.
—Oliver Wendell Holmes

❖ ❖ ❖

Chapter 5

PLUS IT! with Low Moods:
Fifteen Things to Do When Kids Are Feeling Blue

Children have "down" moments when they feel inadequate, unhappy, left out, hurt, or angry. There's nothing wrong with having any of those feelings. But often when we're feeling blue, we really want to let go of the misery and feel cheerful again.

Fortunately, there are many things we can do to feel more sure of ourselves and happy again. So when your kids are down and moody, try one of the *PLUS IT!* techniques below to teach them how to shift back to feeling good about themselves. It's a great gift to children if parents and adults use moments of unhappiness to teach them ways to take care of their emotional responses effectively.

One of the tricks with these ideas is to be sensitive to timing. A child might actually enjoy feeling bad for awhile and may not want to be talked out of it.

But eventually, your child will probably want help to feel better again.

The strategy you pick from the list below will depend on the situation. Sometimes you may want to use several of these suggestions. And, of course, if your child suffers from long-term or deep depression or emotional upset, please seek professional help.

❖   ❖   ❖

You might as well make the most of a bad mood.
—Grandma Anna

The heart of education is the education of the heart.
—Unknown

*The greatest revolution of our generation is
the discovery that human beings, by changing
the inner attitudes of their minds, can
change the outer aspects of their lives.*
—William James

❖   ❖   ❖

1. Breathe Deeply

This is such a simple step, yet it helps! Tell a crying or angry child to take five deep, slow breaths. It changes their focus and relaxes their body. Do the deep breathing along with them.

2. Finish Something That's Been Started

We usually get an energy boost when we complete something. So if your children are feeling low, help them to finish something they started, even if it's just a little thing. For example, they could straighten up their bedroom, complete a homework assignment, put something away, finish a drawing, finish reading a book, and so forth.

3. Acknowledge and Accept It

It is often helpful to ask children to identify what they're feeling. "I'm mad about …" "I'm scared about school." "My feelings are hurt because …"

Let them know that any feeling they have is OK. You can say, "I know what you mean. I've felt that way, too." Often just accepting what they say is enough. You or they may not need a remedy or have to do anything about it. It's just a feeling—and feelings change.

If children are too young to come up with words, say, "It looks to me as though you're feeling sad (or angry or scared)." Giving them words for feelings not only teaches new vocabulary but also helps them find their self-control.

4. Do Something Nice for Someone Else

Being of service to someone else makes us feel useful, and feeling useful brings confidence and self-regard.

Encourage your out-of-sorts child to do something such as make a card for someone's birthday, help prepare supper, change the dog's water, help a brother or sister clean a room, serve a snack to someone, and so forth.

5. Say "I'm Sorry," Forgive Yourself, and Then Forget

We all do things that may hurt others or make them angry, and then we often feel crummy ourselves. A powerful way to change that is to genuinely say, "I'm sorry for …" If you need to do something to correct the situation, do it promptly. Forgive yourself. Then allow yourself to let it go.

Showing children how to admit they did something problematic and then apologize is a great gift. They don't build a storehouse of guilt and resentment.

Teach them that if someone apologizes to them, they can accept it and let it go, too.

If there's not a way to say you're sorry directly to the person involved, it's also powerful to say it to oneself, then let it go.

6. Be Grateful

A marvelous cure for the blues is to focus on things for which you are thankful.

Ask children to name at least five things for which they are grateful. If they have trouble getting started, start with simple physical things: "I'm glad I had cereal

I like for breakfast." "I'm thankful that it's Saturday." "I'm thankful for my friend Billy." If they keep going with this, it's likely their mood will change.

7. Refocus—What Could Be Good about This?

This can be an exceptionally useful question in certain circumstances. When children (and adults) can see one to five possible good things coming out of a situation that seems difficult, they are on their way to restoring emotional balance. For example, if a trip or vacation is cancelled, perhaps that would mean extra money for something else. If a child does poorly on a school test, a positive result may be extra tutoring. But be sensitive about using this question in highly emotional situations such as the death of a pet.

8. Experience Nature

For children and adults, being in nature often restores happiness and calm. Unless being outside is dangerous (for example, if there's a big winter storm brewing), take a walk with an upset child. Or pick flowers in a garden. Kick a soccer ball on the grass. Go to a park. Look at the night sky. Take a drive to the countryside, and get out of the car for a bit. Swim in a pool.

9. Express It—Write about It

Many times we can shift a lousy mood by writing for a few minutes about what's bothering us. Just scribbling fast, not even writing full words, can help. We don't even need to keep what we wrote. In fact, it's best to tear it up, and throw it away without rereading it.

If your children are old enough to write, suggest they try this when they are upset, or let them draw about their feelings.

10. A TV Show in Your Mind: Visualize Something Good

Psychologists tell us that imagining something clearly in your mind is almost as useful as experiencing it. Learning to imagine good things is a tool children can use to calm themselves and get strength in times of stress, confusion, or upset.

Suggest that your children close their eyes and see in their minds a scene they remember or wish for, such as playing with a puppy, running with friends, cuddling up to hear a story read to them, or meeting a fairy princess. Often this can begin to restore balance.

11. Laugh about It

This strategy is not about laughing at a child who is feeling low, but rather, it's about deliberately finding the humor in a situation. If you're going to laugh about it in a week or a month, you might as well laugh about it now. Laughter creates distance from an experience.

You may be surprised to learn that you do not need to be happy to laugh; you do not need jokes or funny situations or comedy routines, although those things can help. People around the world join laughing clubs because even forced laughter helps release tension and create "happy chemistry."

Children and grownups can laugh just because they decide to laugh. Try it. Start with a giggle. Go to a ha-ha. A hee-hee. A ho-ho. Try a belly laugh.

12. Move and Exercise

When we're angry or blue, simply moving our bodies can help change our feelings. Stamping feet up and down *privately* in the kitchen or a bedroom can help release anger and "ground" us; it can bring us out of upsetting emotions. (This works for adults, too.)

Here are other suggestions: Run from one corner of the block to the other. Kick a ball. Shoot baskets. Jog around the block. Take a bike ride. Go to a playground. Dance to music. Go rollerblading or skating. Do jumping jacks or jump rope. Move your body!

13. Get or Give a Hug

Give a hug. Ask for a hug. A back rub is good, too, or an arm around the shoulders, or a gentle hand on the top of the head or the back of the neck.

Boys and girls of all ages need to be touched, appropriately, by adults in their lives. The human touch calms children and helps them focus. Appropriate, love-filled touch helps the brain relax and release the hormones that let us experience joyfulness.

❖   ❖   ❖

We need four hugs a day for survival. We
need eight hugs a day for maintenance. We
need twelve hugs a day for growth.
—Virginia Satir

❖   ❖   ❖

14. Rest

Take a quick nap. It's that simple. Moodiness can be dispelled by slipping into the nap zone, even for a short time. A short sleep can change our whole view of the world.

15. Think of Three Things You Want to Do

Refocusing on what you want, rather than dwelling on what happened, can shift a lousy mood. Ask your child to think of three things they want to do.

❖   ❖   ❖

If you want your children to improve, let them
overhear the nice things you say about them to others.
—Haim Ginott

❖   ❖   ❖

Add your own ideas below for creating cheer:

board. Find out about county or city services from the Internet or library. Ask at the local school. Listen to the local radio station. Watch for interesting ideas on TV public service announcements. Check out what the local churches or temples offer. Start a file for these ideas.

Then pick out and do the activities that appeal to you. Who knows? You might meet engaging neighbors, the kids might make new friends, or you might get invited to a new place!

◆　◆　◆

It is…fun to have things, but more to make them.
—R. J. Baughan

◆　◆　◆

2. Play Indoor and Table Games

These are a great alternative to spending money at video arcades, amusement parks, or other places that require coins and cash.

Try card games that help kids develop alertness and quick-response skills. Depending on the children's ages, play go fish, old maid, slapjack, I doubt it, war, authors, pig, concentration, crazy eights, snap, rolling stone, and so forth. If you need to review how to play these games, look on the Internet or get a games book from the library. Be prepared for noise and fun!

Board games are great. There are dozens of them for all ages: Chutes and Ladders®, Parcheesi®, Sorry®, and of course, the huge favorite, Monopoly®. There are the strategy games, for example, checkers, chess, Chinese checkers, and backgammon. Word games such as Scrabble® and Boggle® engage some children and adults. Plenty of educational board games teach geography, history, and trivia. There are several varieties of domino games and dice games. The table games list is almost endless, and they're oh-so-much fun. If you don't have these games already in your home, search for them at secondhand stores or garage sales.

Then there are thousands of jigsaw puzzles. Completing them requires strategy, focus, and visual skills. Families can be involved with these for days. And there are pencil and paper games: crossword puzzles, acrostics, and sudoku.

Of course, there are also specialized table games such as ping-pong and pool that can take up hours and teach plenty of physical skills.

Use the lined space at the end of this chapter to list the games you enjoy or ones you want to learn.

3. Start a Small Business

Is there something your family or children could make, do, or sell? Homemade greeting cards? Baked goods? Homemade jellies and jams? Sewn, knitted, or crocheted items? Could they prepare a very small community newspaper?

What about a service business: Raking leaves? Providing yard-cleaning services? Car washes? Snow shoveling? Lawn mowing? Delivering newspapers? Shopping for groceries? Providing computer software-use instruction? Babysitting?

4. Organize Physical Activities

Invite friends to join in outside games. How about some of these: Tag. A tree-climbing competition. A track and field day. Basketball. Softball. A jump -rope afternoon. Tennis. Marbles. Jacks. Four-square. Hopscotch. Hide and seek. Capture the flag. Or ball games such as dodge ball and kick ball.

Remember: the priority in physical activities is safety first, then fun.

5. Do an Act of Service

How about a community cleanup day? Could you collect recycling materials? Could you and your children be assistants at a community event, a block party, a town event? Is there a Habitat for Humanity or other nonprofit organization that might use your family's service?

Check into church, temple, YWCA/YMCA, or any religious group's service projects. Are there projects organized by the Boy Scouts or Girl Scouts?

Or tell an elderly neighbor you'd like to help her or him for free in some way—and let that person decide how to use your offer.

6. Plan a No-Cost Party

Doesn't everyone like a spontaneous party or potluck meal? One way to have one is to invite neighbors or friends to your home.

Tell them the One Rule: they must not spend any more money on food or supplies than they'd already planned to use, not even for paper goods. If you or they do not have paper goods in stock, tell folks to bring plates that can be washed before they go home. That's even the more ecological way!

7. Learn Survival Skills

Do you ever wonder how you would manage if, for some reason, you couldn't stay in your own home for a period of time? What if there were an earthquake or fire? Could you and your children find ways to take care of yourselves?

It can be fun (and very wise) to plan what you would do in such an event. Check out library books about wilderness survival or city survival. Learn about edible plants. For example, did you know dandelion leaves are not only edible, but also good for you?

Learn where your community resources are. Take a trip to the fire department, and ask them to teach you what citizens need to know in the event of a fire or natural disaster. If you live in an earthquake-prone area and you don't have an emergency survival kit for your home and your car, create one.

8. Use the Public Library Services

Do your children know how many great things are available for free at the public library? With your children, go to your library with pencils and notebooks in hand. Pretend you are on a treasure hunt, and jointly make a list of the treasures you find there. You may all be surprised.

9. Plan a Spend-No-Money Day or Weekend

For some people, this is a challenge. For others, it's easy. Make it a game to see how long your family can go without buying something. Do you have things sitting in the cupboard or refrigerator that you can cook and eat? Are there toys that have long been neglected? What about reading a book together rather than renting a movie?

Of course, please don't take this to the extreme. If someone needs medication, special supplies, or special food, be sure you take care of their real needs.

10. Have a Scavenger Hunt

It can be an amazing adventure to find what's out there in the world that either nature or people are finished with, such as plastic containers; nuts, bolts, and pipes; cardboard boxes; bottles and caps; furniture pieces; shells, feathers, and seeds, and so forth. Then see what you can invent with your found treasures. Plenty of artists make sculptures with "found objects," and you can get ideas on the Internet or from books in the public library. What could you and your children create?

Add your own ideas below for no-money-needed fun:

_____

_____

_____

_____

_____

_____

_____

_____

_____

_____

_____

Chapter 7

PLUS IT! with TV and Technology

❖　❖　❖

*Television can be turned into a stimulus for your
child's vocabulary development, especially if you
encourage your child to discuss the program.*
—Stan Wonderley, *Success Starts Early*

❖　❖　❖

People talk about how television, computers, and electronic games influence, and may endanger, young minds. Many of us have concerns about children's exposure to violence, inappropriate sexual images, and limited language. We may worry about kids sitting passively before a screen rather than playing creatively and getting exercise. We may worry about their brain development being affected by electromagnetic frequencies. We may worry about the quality of the information they receive from TV and about who controls that information.

Electronics and technology are in our world to stay. And they change all the time. I recommend that you steadfastly limit the amount of time children spend with electronic items and TV, and that you use the *PLUS IT!* activities below to help children benefit from their experiences with technology.

1. Characters You Like

Characters—human, cartoon, or mechanical—are everywhere: in ads, TV shows, and video games. Some are heroes; some are villains.

To do this activity, simply ask your children, "What do you like about _____ character?" Encourage your children to talk about things they noticed, particularly the actions the character took. Ask why the character acted that way.

Help them learn new words for characteristics. If your child says, "_____ was nice," teach new words for nice, such as kind, generous, warm, outgoing, compassionate, caring, gentle, supportive, and sweet. If a child says, "_____ is funny," teach terms such as comical, hilarious, witty, slapstick, and clowning. Don't hesitate to use big words, even with small children. That's exactly how they learn them.

Generally I recommend asking about positive qualities of characters because noticing these contributes to fun, creativity, and energy.

As you talk together, look for opportunities to tell your children when they also demonstrate positive qualities. For example, say something such as, "You know, I thought the comment you made about _____ was witty, too!" We often see in others the positive (and negative) characteristics we ourselves have, and it helps build our self-knowledge and self-regard to have others notice those things in us.

2. Act As If, Impersonate, Pretend, and Make Believe

Kids are natural actors. Try asking your children to act as if they are a favorite TV show or video character. Can you walk like the character walks? Talk like the character? Are there any characteristic phrases the character uses? What about gestures?

This gets them to watch the character carefully, building their skills of observation about human personalities. Do this strictly in fun. Let yourself enjoy any attempts your children make to impersonate a character or speak with their accent or manner. And you try being an actor, too!

3. Retell

Another way to use *PLUS IT!* activities to make watching TV an educational as well as a viewing experience is to ask your kids to retell a story they watched. Listen attentively. Your children may be long-winded and recount every detail, or they may be sketchy. Receive whatever they tell you uncritically.

Retelling a story reinforces their ability to recall, which is a great skill for success in school. It also reveals what they find interesting, puzzling, or valuable.

4. Retell and Revise

Like the activity above, in doing this one, simply ask children whether they would like a different ending for the show or story they watched. Let them tell you what happened and how it could have been different.

5. My Strategies

In playing video and electronic games, children and adults devise strategies to win the race, to beat the clock, to free the hero, to outsmart the computer, and so forth. The more strategies they have, the more fun they have.

Ask children, "What tricks are you using when you play? What works for you? What does not seem to work?" Encourage them to notice what works and what doesn't work—and then to use more of the former and less of the latter. This is a crucial thinking and life skill.

6. Winning and Losing

Good sportsmanship is all about enjoying the game, playing full out, and doing our best. It's not getting hung up on whether we win or lose. This applies to all sorts of games, including electronic ones. Some children understand this automatically; others get upset when they lose. When children get upset with losing, they may inwardly be saying harsh things to themselves, even if they outwardly blame others. They may be thinking things such as, "I'm so stupid or clumsy" or "It wasn't fair."

You can help disappointed children realize that they feel bad because of negative self-talk, which is what they say inside their minds about themselves. To help them become aware of this, you might ask, "What do you say to yourself when you lose?"

Then suggest alternative things to say inwardly, such as, "I'm learning, and mistakes can help me learn. I wonder what can I do differently next time? What do I need more practice in? What did I do well?"

Similar questions can be asked when children are the winners: "What helped you win? How can you do more of that?"

7. Help 'Em Out

Do your children pick up on how to use technological things more quickly than you do? Do they have the patience to use trial-and-error to figure out how to get something to work? If so, ask them to teach you or coach you.

When we teach something to someone else, everybody learns. The "teacher" learns about how other people's minds work, where there are misunderstandings and how to correct them, and where there are weaknesses in skills and how to strengthen them. They can also learn the value of encouragement. The "student" can learn new information and skills, how to continue trying, and how to ask questions. It's a win-win.

Add your own ideas below for learning from television, video, and technology:

_____

_____

_____

_____

_____

_____

_____

_____

_____

_____

_____

Chapter 8

Not everyone considers cleaning and maintaining a house as drudgery, but housework tends to have that reputation. Nevertheless, it has to be done.

Children need to know how to care for themselves and their things, so here are ideas to help kids learn.

You've probably noticed that some creative, productive people are sloppy. They have stuff strewn all over their space, yet they find what they need and accomplish what they want. On the other hand, some organized, tidy people spend so much of their time cleaning up, they don't accomplish what they say they want to do. I believe there isn't a right and wrong in this area, but there are more helpful and less helpful ways to live. Generally speaking, orderliness and cleanliness help children and adults feel more cared for, energetic, happy, and calm.

Two skills that are important for children to learn are:

* How to do things to take care of themselves
* How to cooperate with others around them

These things are best taught patiently, over time, by expecting them of children, and by adults setting the example.

◆ ◆ ◆

You have a lifetime to work, but
children are only young once.
—Polish Proverb

◆ ◆ ◆

1. Make a List

This is easy. Together with your children, write down all the housework and family maintenance activities you can think of.

Here are some common ones to get you started. Cross off ones that don't apply to your situation, and add others that do:

* Shopping for groceries
* Making beds
* Vacuuming
* Washing dishes
* Cooking
* Dusting

* Picking up toys or papers
* Babysitting
* Sweeping the porch or driveway
* Raking leaves
* Weeding the garden
* Washing clothes
* Folding clothes
* Ironing clothes
* Bringing in the mail
* Emptying wastebaskets
* Taking out the garbage or trash
* Shoveling snow
* Washing the car
* Putting gas in the car
* Watering plants

Put your list somewhere safe, and continue to add to it over time. Once you have a long list, you can use it in many ways: to plan your weekends, to assign chores to family members, to leave instructions for a house-sitter or neighbor when you go on vacation, and so forth.

Children often forget their jobs. Adults forget them, too. When kids participate in creating such a list, they learn a simple way to remind themselves of things that need to be handled. It helps them learn to plan their time and activities.

2. The Fun of Finishing

Have you ever done a task but left a small, final detail uncompleted? Maybe you didn't put away the sweeper after vacuuming the room, or you didn't take out the full can of trash after cleaning the kitchen, or you didn't put away the clean laundry after you folded it.

We all do this from time to time. Does your mind nag you about that little something that still needs to be done? When you see it again, do you think, "Oh, no. Now I've got to do that!"

Great satisfaction comes from getting something done *completely*, whether it's homework, housework, or job work. People feel relieved, energetic, and happy when something is totally finished. Gently support your children in finishing for the fun of it! This teaches them to persist—an all-important skill that supports accomplishment and success.

3. A Place for Everything

There's a simple way to help children learn to become organized and take responsibility for their schoolwork and their toys—have a place where each thing belongs: their books, toys, lunch boxes, papers, pens and pencils, clothing, shoes, coats, and so forth. Everything.

Choose a good location for things, get appropriate containers for them, and then put them there!

Gently and consistently remind children where things go if they forget, and over time keeping things in place will become a habit. If things "walk" to other locations over time, have a clutter-removal hour once a week or so, and get the whole family to participate in returning things to where they belong.

4. Health and Housework: How These Things Relate

You can frequently teach children about healthy and safe practices as you go through the week. For example, when they are old enough, children can take out food and other trash to the appropriate place. Remind them that this task has to do with preventing insects and rodents from sharing your home with you.

Similarly, as you recycle plastics, glass, paper, batteries, and other used household materials, explain how recycling helps the planet and creates jobs.

Keeping rugs vacuumed, surfaces dusted, and floors reasonably clean can help relieve allergies. When children know their health is affected, there is additional motivation to do the best thing.

5. Make Life Easier: The Right Tool

Have you ever tried to open a can with a jackknife, or put plain paper into a three-ring binder by using the open rings to punch the holes in the paper? You can do it, but it's harder, and it may not look good.

One wonderful thing to teach kids is that there is a tool for just about every need. Creative, practical people have invented devices to help with almost every problem.

When your children attempt to do something such as cut cardboard with a kitchen knife or glue a broken plate together with tape, you can *PLUS* these experiences by helping them find a tool that does the job easily and correctly.

Take your children to hardware and home supply stores or to hobby shops to teach them that tools are available to help them make and do things. You don't need to buy every tool—sometimes you can borrow them from neighbors, or rent them from stores. However, special tools are great as birthday gifts, or suggest children save their allowances to buy tools for themselves.

Show children how to use tools safely and how to care for them. Have a place for every tool or piece of equipment, and teach children to put it back there.

6. Maintaining Tools and Equipment

A great way to *PLUS IT!* when you're doing housework with children is to show them the proper maintenance of materials, tools, appliances, or equipment. When they are at an appropriate age, show them how to keep household items functioning well. Here's a list of things you may want to show children how to do:

✱ Dust electronic equipment
✱ Empty vacuum sweepers

* Sharpen knives
* Change water pitcher filters
* Clean crumbs from a toaster
* Insert beater paddles
* Wrap cords
* Let an iron cool
* Clean a fan
* Tighten loose screws
* Change a light bulb

Both girls and boys need to know all about tools and how to use and maintain them!

7. Caring for Plants

Most of us enjoy live plants in our homes. They provide beauty, color, oxygen, and freshness.

Involve your children in plant care: watering plants, providing good containers, picking off dead leaves, moving plants to proper lighting, selecting plants in a store, repotting them, and so forth.

You can *PLUS* these activities by teaching kids the names of plants. If you don't know the names yourself, that's not a problem. Show children how to find out information. Check out a library book on common plants. Go on the Internet to learn more. Take your children to a florist shop, and speak with the employees or owner.

Add a new plant name to your (and your children's) vocabulary whenever possible. If needed, put a little label on the plant to help yourselves remember its name.

8. Caring for Pets

Parents often get pets in order to teach children about caring for live animals. Different kinds of pets need different kinds of care.

The basic care areas are these:

* Feeding—what to feed, when to feed, how much to feed, how to keep food clean
* Bathroom practices—providing a place and time for the animal to go to the bathroom, proper cleanup, how to avoid odors
* Legal regulations—for example, a dog license
* Medical/physical care—shots or neutering or flea-prevention as needed, bathing, exercise
* Safety—fences, closed doors, clipped nails
* Training—where is the animal allowed or prohibited, what behaviors are expected
* Respect for the animal—kindness, protection

Undoubtedly, there are many more ways to use housework to teach important life skills to kids.

Add your own ideas below for making housework an educational experience:

5. Is there somebody else I should tell or ask about it?

6. How is it fun or valuable?

7. Can I afford it in terms of money, time, and energy?

8. What might this lead to next?

9. Who will it help?

10. What other choices do I have?

Add your own questions below:

_____

_____

_____

_____

_____

_____

_____

_____

_____

_____

Chapter 10

PLUS IT! in a Car:
Ten Ways to Use Travel Time

Kids and parents often spend huge amounts of time together in cars, buses, or subways. Over the years, that time together could add up to many days of confinement in those little spaces. Here are *PLUS IT!* ideas to make those minutes and hours together lively, loving, and filled with learning.

An essential piece of equipment for those who use automobiles is a Car Notebook. This can be a simple lined notebook or a blank book. Clip a pen on it, and keep them both together in the car.

Or better yet, prepare a Car Box with a clipboard, several pens and pencils, the notebook, a local map, and a book to read. You may want to also include a flashlight and a compass. Keep this box in the car at all times!

1. Books on Tape, CD, iPods, or Other Players

There are hundreds of great books out there, and you'll never have time to read them all. An obvious way to *PLUS IT!* on the road is to listen to books on tape or CD (usually available in libraries) or downloaded from the Internet. Select a book everyone in the car is interested in reading, and play it when you're in the car together.

Of course, with iPods and other recording devices, each person could listen to his or her own choice—but I recommend that, when possible, you all listen to the same book over the main amplifier system. Talk about it as you go. Which characters do you like best? What are you learning? Would you like to live in the story?

2. Observation Games

Playing observation games when riding on a highway is fun.

Vanity Plates: One game is to spot and figure out what vanity license tags—tags with a message—say. If your children are of writing age, let them start a page in your Car Notebook just for those license plates. Make three columns. In the first column, write down the license plate spelling. In the next column, write what you think is the meaning. Sometimes you may not be able to figure them out right away, but write them down anyway. In the third column, write the date you saw it.

On another page in your Car Notebook, start a list of your own vanity plate ideas. Over time you and the children will probably have lots of new ideas.

Road Signs Game: On any route you frequently take, let the children count highway department road signs. How many "Emergency Phone," "Speed Limit," "Curve Ahead," "Pedestrian Crossing," or other signs do you see? Have you seen any misspelled signs or out-of-date ones?

3. Backseat Read-Aloud

If a child in the backseat is comfortable reading aloud, ask him or her to read to the driver. You could choose short newspaper or magazine articles about your community, or choose longer books. Choose only those materials that the child is comfortable reading.

4. Backseat Navigator

It's excellent to teach map-reading skills when they are relevant—that is, when you're going someplace. Leave a set of local and state maps in your Car Box. Fold them so they can be read easily, and ask your children to follow on the map the road you're driving.

You can call out the street names as you pass them, and have the children locate them on the map.

If you have a GPS device, check its accuracy by watching a paper map as well. Could there be a shorter way to where you're going?

5. How Far?

Do you know how far it is from your house to school? To the grocery store? To the church, gym, mall, or other location? Ask your child to estimate the distance, and you do the same. Then set your trip meter to check.

In your Car Notebook, start a page titled "How Far?" Make three columns. Label the first, "From"; the second "To"; and the third, "Distance." Then keep track of mileage from place to place—just for the fun of it.

6. Fill 'er Up!

In the days before self-serve gas stations, a common phrase gas station attendants heard was "Fill 'er up!" Now when you get a receipt for a gas purchase, let the children record the amount of gas in the Car Notebook.

Teach them how to figure the MPG (miles per gallon) that your car gets, even if you have a device that does that automatically.

An easy way to do that is this:

a. When you get a full tank of gas, reset your trip meter at zero.

b. The next time you get a full tank of gas, record how many gallons you bought (for example, 15.5 gallons) and the number of miles on the trip meter (for example, 434 miles).

c. Divide the number of miles by the number of gallons (434 divided by 15.5). The answer is that you got 28 miles per gallon.

7. Car Care

Is your car spotless outside and immaculate inside? Or does it look like a deserted picnic table right after a fair, with plastic cups and litter scattered about? Or is your car cleanliness somewhere between those extremes?

Use car-care tasks as *PLUS IT!* opportunities for children. When you go to an auto products store, involve them in the question of which cleanser or wax to purchase. Read the labels together. When you wash the car, either by hand or by machine, let them participate in drying the car.

If you self-check the air pressure in the tires, show them how the gauge works. If you have this done in a service facility, ask the mechanic or clerk to explain to your children how it all works.

When possible, use the correct names for auto parts—air filter, carburetor, transmission, battery, oil pump, and so forth. As children become familiar with the parts of vehicles, they gain knowledge and a sense of competence.

8. Bus, Train, or Subway Options

If you use public transportation, there are plenty of ways to *PLUS IT!* when you're riding with children.

It only takes a little planning to make rides both fun and educational.

Most public transportation systems have printed schedules. You can easily teach your children to read these. They might enjoy it if you quiz them. "According to the schedule, if we leave X-spot at 9:30, when would we get to Y-spot?" Compare a schedule of stopping points with a conventional map. Can your child find the bus or train stops on the conventional map?

Is there a bus driver or train conductor you might get to know? If your child asks politely, and at a time that's safe, that person may be willing to talk about his or her job. What qualifications are needed to get the job? Does the driver have stories of unusual riders? What's great about the job?

As with car travel, reading is often a great choice while riding public transportation. Help your children develop the habit of putting a book or magazine in their school bags or purses so they have something to read during a ride.

9. What's Around Here?

Both car and public transportation riders pass places worthy of notice. But sometimes we don't even realize what's interesting in our town or environment. Tourists often come from far away to see things that local people never visit!

There are ways to *PLUS IT!* so children become aware of their surroundings and local treasures.

Start a page in your Car Notebook entitled "What's Around Here." As you pass public buildings or places in the course of daily life, have the children write the building names and addresses.

For example, can they locate the post office, water department, electric company, library, city hall, social services office, hospital, clinic, jail, city or county parks, police station, and fire station?

Notice privately owned establishments, too. How many restaurants are in your area? How many of those are Chinese, Japanese, Thai, Indian, fast food? How many banks are there? Malls? Grocery stores? Schools? Churches?

And are there any tourist spots? Museums? Sports arenas?

Your children's lists of "What's Around Here" could grow quite long. On days when you don't have much to do, visit some of those places. Find out what happens there.

10. Highway Reporter

Some kids love to imitate the voices and styles of radio or TV newscasters. Encourage them to play like that. When you pass something unusual or eventful as you drive, invite them to report it on the spot. It could be a fire, an accident, new construction, a store closing, a school announcement, a playground ball game in session, or anything else of note. For example, "This is Martin, reporting live from the playground."

If your children like to write, suggest they write the story as if for a newspaper. They could read it at home to other family members. Not only does an activity like this help kids learn about their community, but it also gives them practice in putting words together in interesting ways.

Add your own ideas for making travel time interesting and fun:

_____

_____

_____

_____

_____

_____

_____

_____

_____

_____

_____

_____

Chapter II

PLUS IT! at the Table:
Supper Conversation Starters

A great place and time to have conversations is when family members are eating together, whether as a group or just as two or three.

❖ ❖ ❖

The more often children and teens eat dinner with their families, the less likely they are to smoke, drink, or use drugs.

—From research by the National Center on Addiction and Substance Abuse at Columbia University

❖ ❖ ❖

Sometimes kids are full of talk and laughter; at other times they're quiet. You can often open up or direct conversations by using a starter-question

87

such as the ones below. Sometimes these sorts of questions seem a little artificial, yet they give kids the opportunity to reflect and to think about things in a bigger way. Experience with reflection, thinking, and answering questions are useful skills for school.

Pick the conversation starters you like, or make up your own conversation prompts. If you do this from time to time (perhaps once a week), your children will get used to answering this type of question. Be sure to answer the questions for yourself, too. As your children get used to this format, let whatever they say be OK. If a child wants to pass, that's fine, too. (And of course, you can use these at any time of the day, not just at the dinner table.)

Turn off the TV or radio when you talk together so that everyone gets full attention. For further ideas on ways to stimulate conversation with children, go to www.familylearningjournal.com and click on "Supper-Time Talk."

❖ ❖ ❖

Each day of our lives we make deposits in
the memory banks of our children.
—Charles R. Swindoll

❖ ❖ ❖

1. "Round Robin*: What's on Your Mind Today that You'd Like to Share?"

2. "What Did You Discover Today?"

3. "Something Good that Happened Today"

4. "Something I'm Grateful For"

5. "Tell Us about [School, an Activity, a Person, etc.]"

6. "You Don't Like the Food? Let's Plan a Menu"

7. "One of My Strengths [or One of Your Strengths]"

8. "Something I Like about You"

9. "Something I Like about Me"

10. "Something I'd Like to Ask for Help With..."

11. "A Mistake I Made Today (and Laugh about It)"

12. "What Do You Think We Should Do About (Any Problem)?"

* A round robin is simply going around in a circle to let everyone have a chance to say something. In a round robin, if someone doesn't want to talk when it's their turn, they can just say "Pass."

Add your own ideas below for stimulating conversation:

_____

_____

_____

_____

_____

_____

_____

_____

_____

_____

_____

_____

_____

_____

_____

_____

_____

Chapter 12

How to Transform Ordinary Activities into Educational Ones

Sometimes people ask, "How can I think of ideas for things to do with my kids? It's so easy to just turn on the TV or get stuck in routines."

Or they say, "I'd really like to do more active things with them, but there just isn't time for me to handle my home responsibilities, plus my job, and have energy left over to do educational things with the kids."

The answer: Just keep looking for opportunities to *PLUS IT!* as you go through your day. They'll show up! Here are the *PLUS IT!* steps:

* Notice
* Talk and Listen
* *PLUS IT!*—Do Something Deliberate with the Activity

91

1. Notice

Notice what you're already doing in your daily life. I mean things such as going to the store, walking to a neighbor's home, getting the mail from the mailbox, using the stove, putting laundry into the washing machine, brushing your teeth, walking the dog, changing kitty litter, driving the car, getting on a bus, cleaning the bathroom. You can probably list hundreds more.

Once you start noticing the daily activities you do automatically, you'll be able to see and create *PLUS IT!* opportunities easily.

2. Talk and Listen

Talk to your children as you go through the day. About what? About the things you've noticed; about almost everything (except, of course, inappropriate "adult" things). Just know that it's far better to use too many big words with children rather than not enough.

Sometimes parents don't talk to babies or toddlers much because the children can't yet answer in return. But kids learn through hearing. So chat, chat, chat with them! Talk about the five Ws and a How—who, what, when, where, why, how. This helps them gain information and vocabulary and learn about the give-and-take conventions of conversation.

Here are some examples of what to talk about:

WHO: "You know, your new babysitter has four brothers and sisters and is on the school basketball team. She's a very active person."

WHAT the order of activities is: "I like to wipe off the table first so that any crumbs fall to the floor before I sweep it."

WHEN: "On the weekend I'll have time to take you to the library to check out some books. I'm looking forward to that because I want to get a book for myself, too."

WHERE: "The store we're going to is on the north side of the street. In our town, north is in the direction of the big mountains."

WHY you're doing things: "I'm putting carrots in this salad because they add fiber to our diet, and our bodies need fiber to function properly."

HOW: "When I cook rice, I put one cup of grain and a cup and a half of water into the pot. That's what the directions say to do."

Then listen when your children talk. All kids are different from one another. In the same family there can be chatty David, who talks endlessly about his ideas, and quiet Emily, who rarely says a word.

I recommend you listen attentively to a talkative child, and if it gets to be too much, you can simply say, "I can't be a good listener right now because I need to pay attention to _____. Let's talk about this more tomorrow."

For the quiet ones, I recommend you ask them questions that require more than a yes or no answer. Good ways to start such a question are "Tell me about ..." or "What do you think about ...?"

3. *PLUS IT!*—Do Something Deliberate with the Activity

In the preceding chapters are examples of doing something deliberate with any ordinary, everyday activity. You can:

* Write it
* Count it
* Draw it
* List it
* Time it
* Compare it
* Collect it
* Report it
* Discuss it
* Clean it
* Observe it
* Investigate it
* Make it up

* Alter it
* Memorize it
* And more!

I invite you to use these suggestions as inspiration to invent your own. Of course, what activities you do depends on the age and temperament of your children. Be sensible and sensitive, making modifications as appropriate. Do what works! And most importantly, enjoy it!

◆　◆　◆

The essence of intelligence is skill in extracting meaning from everyday experience.
—Unknown

◆　◆　◆

Bonus Offer! FREE!

For FIVE rewarding Family Activities, go to

<www.PlusItBook.com>

Click on SPECIAL BONUS! It's a gift to you.

You'll find simple instructions for five no-cost and fun things you can do with your family—whether your family has many members or just two.

You can print out these activities. Do one each month for the next five months. Enjoy!

No additional purchase is required.

Come visit <www.PlusItBook.com> now!

About the Author

Esther A. Jantzen, Ed.D., worked for twenty-five years in urban public school systems. She believes an important way to improve academic achievement in America is through creating stronger bonds between the home and the school, because parents are a child's most important teachers. She creates educational materials designed to inspire, encourage, and inform parents, caregivers, and teachers.

Jantzen lives in Southern California, only a forty-five-minute drive (when it's not rush hour) from her grandchildren.

For additional information, see

www.PlusItBook.com.

BUY A SHARE OF THE FUTURE IN YOUR COMMUNITY

These certificates make great holiday, graduation and birthday gifts that can be personalized with the recipient's name. The cost of one S.H.A.R.E. or one square foot is $54.17. The personalized certificate is suitable for framing and will state the number of shares purchased and the amount of each share, as well as the recipient's name. The home that you participate in "building" will last for many years and will continue to grow in value.

HABITAT FOR HUMANITY

THIS CERTIFIES THAT

YOUR NAME HERE

HAS INVESTED IN A HOME FOR A DESERVING FAMILY

1985-2005

TWENTY YEARS OF BUILDING FUTURES IN OUR
COMMUNITY ONE HOME AT A TIME

1200 SQUARE FOOT HOUSE @ $65,000 = $54.17 PER SQUARE FOOT
This certificate represents a tax deductible donation. It has no cash value.

Here is a sample SHARE certificate:

YES, I WOULD LIKE TO HELP!

*I support the work that Habitat for Humanity does and I want to be part of the excitement! As a donor, I will receive periodic updates on your construction activities but, more importantly, I know my gift will help a family in our community realize the dream of homeownership. **I would like to SHARE in your efforts against substandard housing in my community!** (Please print below)*

PLEASE SEND ME _____ SHARES at $54.17 EACH = $ $_____

In Honor Of: _____

Occasion: (Circle One)   HOLIDAY   BIRTHDAY   ANNIVERSARY

OTHER: _____

Address of Recipient: _____

Gift From: _____   *Donor Address:* _____

Donor Email: _____

I AM ENCLOSING A CHECK FOR $ $_____ PAYABLE TO HABITAT FOR HUMANITY OR PLEASE CHARGE MY VISA OR MASTERCARD *(CIRCLE ONE)*

Card Number _____   Expiration Date: _____

Name as it appears on Credit Card _____   Charge Amount $ _____

Signature _____

Billing Address _____

Telephone # Day _____   Eve _____

PLEASE NOTE: Your contribution is tax-deductible to the fullest extent allowed by law.
Habitat for Humanity • P.O. Box 1443 • Newport News, VA 23601 • 757-596-5553
www.HelpHabitatforHumanity.org

Printed in the USA
CPSIA information can be obtained
at www.ICGtesting.com
JSHW082221140824
68134JS00015B/659

9 781600 375668